Contents

INTRODUCTION i
1. What is this guidebook about? i
2. Who should read this guidebook? i
3. Objectives of this guidebook i
4. How to use this guidebook? i

PART I – YOU AS A START-UP ENTREPRENEUR 1
1. Do you have what it takes to be an entrepreneur? 1
2. Which type and field of business is more suitable for you? 4
   - 2.1. Field of business 6
   - 2.2. Type of business 6
   - 2.3. Identify your business field and type 7
3. How to strengthen your entrepreneurial abilities and skills? 8

PART II – THE MARKET IS READY ARE YOU? 11
1. Your business idea 11
2. What makes a business idea? 13
   - 2.1 Which need will your business fulfill for the customers? 13
   - 2.2 What good or service will your business sell? 15
   - 2.3 Who will your business sell to? 17
   - 2.4 How is your business going to sell its goods or services? 18
   - 2.5 How much will your business depend on and impact the environment? 19

PART III – GENERATE SMALL BUSINESS IDEAS LIST 23
1. Sean's experience 23
2. How to identify your own list of business ideas? 25
3. Learn from successful business owners 26

4. Draw from experience ... 31
    4.1 Your own experience ... 31
    4.2 Other people's experience. ... 31
5. Survey your local business area ... 33
6. Scanning your environment ... 37
    6.1 Natural resources ... 37
    6.2 Abilities and skills of people in the local community ... 38
    6.3 Waste products ... 39
    6.4 Import substitution ... 40
    6.5 Publications ... 40
    6.6 Trade fairs and exhibitions ... 41
7. Brainstorming ... 43
8. Structured brainstorming ... 44
9. Your ideas list ... 47

PART IV - THE BEST BUSINESS IDEAS FOR YOU ... 49

1. Screen your ideas list ... 49
2. Field study ... 53
    4.2 Conducting your interviews ... 53
    4.2 Who to talk to? ... 53
3. SWOT analysis ... 55
    3.1 Inside the business ... 55
    3.2 Outside the business ... 56

PART V - GENERATE SMALL BUSINESS IDEAS ... 61

INTRODUCTION

1. What is this guidebook about?

In this guidebook we will discuss the basic requirements that are needed to be an entrepreneur, the capabilities that an entrepreneur needs to have and the ways that he or she can come up with a good business idea.

2. Who should be reading this guidebook?

This guidebook is helpful for any potential entrepreneur who wants to start a business, but is not sure of which business idea to pursue.

3. Objectives of this guidebook

When you have completed this guidebook, you should be able to:

- Assess whether or not you have the basic requirements needed to be a successful entrepreneur
- Clearly explain any business idea that comes to your mind
- Identify potential sources of business ideas and create an idea list
- Shortlist and then select the best idea to pursue in order to start your own business/es

4. How to use this guidebook?

In this guidebook you will find:

- **Stories of businesses:** Compare these examples with your own business and use them to improve the performance and profitability of your business.
- **Activities:** Practical exercises in the middle of each part that help you to proactively think about the concepts and how to apply them to your future business.
- **Assessments:** Answering the questions will help you to assess your capability and readiness to become an entrepreneur.
- **Action Plans:** Fill in and use the Action Plans at the end of some parts. These will help you to put your new knowledge into practice.

Several icons are used within the guidebook to help guide your study. Examples of the icons and their meanings are listed below:

When you see this icon, you have activities to do or questions to answer.

When you see this icon, you have to complete assessments that help you measure your capability and readiness to become an entrepreneur.

When you see this icon, it tells you where to find more information or what to do.

PART I

YOU AS A START-UP ENTREPRENEUR

Are you excited thinking about owning and running a business yourself? While it sounds very tempting, being an entrepreneur also means taking on a lot of responsibilities and facing a lot of challenges!

First of all, you need to find out if you are capable of running your own business. Favourable circumstances, in combination with certain personal characteristics and skills are necessary elements for your development as a successful entrepreneur. You will also need specific knowledge and experience in the field to be ultimately successful in the business you choose.

Below are two assessments that you should make before going into business. The first one will measure whether you have the right abilities to be an entrepreneur. The second assessment will help you to identify which type and field of business may be suitable for you.

1. Do you have what it takes to be an entrepreneur?

ASSESSMENT

The following assessment will help you find out if you have the basic requirements of an entrepreneur. Be honest when you answer the questions.

Think about each of the following factors presented as questions. If you answer YES to the questions dealing with any particular factor, consider that factor as one of your strengths. If you answer NO to most of the questions or you are not quite sure about the answers, those factors may be areas that need improvement before you start your business – in which case you will need a mentor.

Personal characteristics, skills and your situation	AREAS OF STRENGTH	AREAS THAT NEED IMPROVEMENT
Passion Are you passionate about running your own business? Is it very meaningful and important to you, your family and the community? Are you enthusiastic about making your business a success and are you willing to put it before almost everything else?	Yes ☐	No ☐

Goal orientation

Are you able to see the big picture and to create clear goals for your business? Are you determined to direct all of your endeavours towards achieving your goals?

Making decisions

When you are confronted with a difficult situation, are you able to keep calm, seek adequate information and make important decisions without postponing or passing the problem on to someone else?

Taking risks

There is no absolutely safe business idea. You always run the risk of failure. Are you aware of the risks and do you accept the possibility that your business might fail? Have you sought adequate information so that you can honestly estimate how big a risk you are going to take?

Ability to handle stress

Entrepreneurs are subjected to a lot of stress when making difficult decisions, managing different business stakeholders and working long hours. Are you able to maintain a positive spirit under pressure? Can you see opportunities in difficult situations?

Social support

Running your business will take a lot of time and effort. Will you get adequate support from family, friends and other business people?

Financial situation

Access to financial resources to start your business is important. Have you set some money aside to get your business started? Do you have family or friends who might be willing and able to lend you money? Do you have a savings or credit history with a financial institution that provides start-up loans?

Business management skills

Business management skills are the ability to run your business efficiently. Are you good in some business management areas, such as marketing, sales, costing or staff motivation, etc.?

☐ ☐

Commitment to your community

An entrepreneur plays an important role in the development of the community. Are you aware of this role? Are you committed to the social advancement of the community as a whole?

☐ ☐

| Number of areas where you are strong | Number of areas needing improvement |

Count the number of strengths and areas of improvements you listed above and write the total here.

☐ ☐

ACTIVITY 1

Look at the assessment areas above and decide which ones that need improvement and growth are critical for your business success. Make a note of them in the box below:

Critical areas needing improvement and growth:
....
....
....
....
....
....
....

If you choose a business based on your work experience, technical skills, knowledge of business practices, hobbies, social ties and family background, etc., there is a greater chance that you will succeed.

Consider the following examples:

Darryle has been working for a courier company for many years. He learned how to manage the courier business and how to develop the required networks. He is considering opening up his own courier service to operate in his country and the East African region.

Maria has grown up in a farmer's family. Her parents grow seasonal vegetables to sell to the local retailers. Maria has graduated from the Agricultural College. She knows various planting techniques and is enthusiastic about promoting the planting, sales and consumption of organic foods in her community. Maria decides to grow organic vegetables on her parents' farm and to sell the products through their retail network.

Kim loves fashion. While she was a student in the capital city, Kim went shopping and discovered a source of inexpensive imported clothes and accessories. She has now returned to her hometown. She decides to buy fashion items from that source and resell to fashion shops in her area.

Jean worked for a construction materials company for several years. He is very familiar with all the brands and knows the quality of various construction materials. When repairing his house last year, he realized that there was no shop in the area selling the supplies he needed. He decides to open a shop near his home, selling all types of basic construction materials, such as cement, bricks, tiles, sand, paint, etc. He enjoys meeting people and advising them about the different types of construction materials.

Below is a summary of how the people in the examples above have chosen their field and type of business:

Field of business	Manufacturing	Service provision	Wholesaling	Retailing
Agriculture	MARIA's vegetable farm			
Construction				JEAN's construction materials shop
Transportation		Darryle's courier service		
Garment			KIM's wholesale clothes shop	
.... (many more)				

Type of business

In the following section, we will further explain what fields of business and types of business exist before suggesting those that will be most suitable for you.

2.1 Field of business

A field of business refers to an industrial category, such as farming, fishing, food processing, garments, construction, furniture, beauty salon, stationery, etc. Your talent, family background, experience, hobbies or interests often inspire you to develop a certain field of business. Your decision to pursue a particular field of business should also match your knowledge, skills and situation.

2.2 Type of business

A type of business identifies how you take part in the business field that you choose. Your personal characteristics and your available networks often guide you into a suitable type of business.

There are four main types of businesses:

- Manufacturing

Manufacturers are businesses that use raw materials, such as leather, waste material, wood, cloth or metal and make new or different products out of those materials. Some examples of manufacturing businesses are shoemakers, dressmakers, furniture makers, paper producers and farm equipment manufacturers. If you know how to produce a good and to make something that is in demand and valuable to customers, you may want to go into manufacturing.

- Service Provision

Service providers are people whose businesses sell a particular service, such as transportation, tours, hairdressing, banking, deliveries, construction, repairs, cleaning, painting, nursing, mentorship, etc. If you enjoy working with people and satisfying their specific needs, providing services may be your forte.

- Wholesaling

Wholesalers are businesses that buy large quantities of certain goods from manufacturers and resell those goods to retail outlets, who then resell them to individual consumers. If you are familiar with companies that make and sell their goods in bulk and you are good at establishing relationships with retailers, you may want to be a wholesaler.

- Retailing

Retailers purchase ready-made goods from wholesalers or suppliers for resale at a profit. Some examples of retail businesses are grocery stores, appliance stores, clothing stores, stationery shops, computer and mobile phone shops, etc. If you like meeting different people and you have access to a good location to open a shop, retailing may be a good option for you.

2.3 Identify your business field and type

ASSESSMENT

The following assessment helps you to identify the field and type of business that you should opt for. Be honest in your assessment. List at least 5 of each.

1. My interests – I enjoy doing the following (include your hobbies):	Possible business fields:
2. My experience – I have worked in or have educational experience in the following field(s) of business (list jobs, training and other sources of work experience):	
3. My business network – I know the following people, friends and relatives who are in business and who could provide information, advice or assistance (state their position):	Possible business types:
4. My preference is to: •• Work with a lot of people/work on my own •• Be active and work outdoors/work at the desk all day •• Do physical work/work in a job that allows me to be creative/do work that requires logical thinking •• Focus on technical details/talk to and care for people	

Remember that this assessment can direct you into the business field and type for which you are best suited. You can always return to this assessment, rethink the choice that you have made and make a different decision.

3. How to strengthen your entrepreneurial abilities and skills?

What if you do not have all the desired characteristics and skills to be an entrepreneur or if your situation is not right to be an entrepreneur at this time? Look at the assessment areas above and identify the areas that need improvement and growth, which are critical for you to start your business and succeed in it. There are many ways to improve your entrepreneurial abilities. You can:

- Learn from people who run their own business, especially those in your chosen business field and type
- Attend training courses
- Find work as an assistant or apprentice in a successful business in the field and type that you are interested in
- Read articles about businesses in your field and type in newspapers and trade journals, either on the internet or at libraries to help you think about the problems these businesses are facing and their proposed solutions
- Join a small business association in your area and participate in forums
- Set aside small amounts of money on a daily or weekly basis to help finance your new business
- Develop the skills and attitudes described below by applying them in your daily activities:
  — Increase your motivation and commitment by making a plan for your future
  — When things go wrong, analyze what happened and improve your ability to learn from mistakes
  — Accept the problems, assess the solutions and take risks
  — Become more open to new ideas and other people's views

You might want to think about finding a partner who complements your abilities, instead of going into business entirely on your own. A partner might also be able to bring financial resources, collateral or relationships with financial service providers that could be helpful if your business ever needed a loan.

There are a number of successful business people who did not have much experience or practice in their particular field or type of business before starting their companies. What is important is to be aware of the areas that need improvement and develop a plan of action to deal with these before they negatively affect your business. Complete the Action Plan on the next page to help you assess how you intend to improve your knowledge, skills and business situation.

ACTIVITY 2

ACTION PLAN		
Areas that need improvement	What will I do to improve it?	When?

PART II

THE MARKET IS READY ARE YOU?

1. Your business idea

Janet's experience

Janet has a small farm and her husband works in a nearby mine, but even though both of them have jobs, they do not earn enough money to pay for their children's education.

Janet decides to try and start her own business by rearing chickens to sell. She knows how to do it and her uncle gives her a loan of R40 000 to start the business. However, before she buys the chicks, someone tells her that there is a huge demand for sunflower oil because of its lack of availability in the market. Traders are knocking on the doors of local farmers asking them to produce it. Thinking she can earn a lot more money from pressing sunflower seeds for oil, Janet changes her business idea and starts an oil pressing venture.

Janet has never grown a large quantity of sunflowers. She spends all the money from the loan to buy seeds, fertilizer and the oil pressing equipment. Since she uses most of the family farmland to grow sunflowers, there is less land to grow maize and vegetables for the family to eat.

The chemicals from the fertilizer begin to make her children sick. She now also has to buy more food for the family. It takes a lot of time and effort to process the oil, so, Janet has to employ someone to help her. A lot of other farmers have started growing sunflower seeds too. Therefore, by the time her oil is ready to sell, the market is already saturated with the goods and Janet cannot find a buyer. To reduce her losses, Janet has to sell the oil at a very low price to a local shop. As a result, Janet makes very little money and she is not able to pay back the loan.

What is wrong with Janet's business idea? Why?

_____
_____
_____

Now look at another case:

Karin's experience

Karin had been working in the assembly line of a garment factory for more than five years. Her salary was low and she was often required to work overtime. 's sister-in-law came to visit and complained to that she was unable to find any good clothes for her 12 year-old daughter. She said that the clothes in the stores all seem to be either made for younger children or for adults. After the visit, decided to go around to the clothing shops in her town. She saw young teenage girls shopping in the stores, but she noticed that the number and variety of clothes geared to that age group was limited. She had already been thinking of quitting her job and opening her own business.

Therefore, decides to design some pretty clothes and dresses for young teenage girls. She makes some drawings of clothing that would appeal to that age group. She then takes her drawings to the local clothing shops, asking the owners if they would buy the dresses in the drawings, how much they would pay for them and how many they would buy. The shop owners seemed to be quite happy with her designs and said they would display her clothes. Then uses her savings to buy a sewing machine and some material to make her first batch. She works in the evening after getting off from work at the garment factory. All of the dresses she makes sell very well and the shops are willing to pay her in cash upon delivery. then decides to quit her job to focus on her own business. Within six months, starts receiving regular orders from the shops. She plans to buy one more sewing machine and hire one of her friends to work for her.

Why is Karin successful in her own business? What did she do that made her successful?

_____
_____
_____

Starting a business is not an easy job. It takes a lot of work and a lot of planning. The effort and the money it takes to start a business may be lost if you do not start the right business. The right business begins with a good description of your business idea.

2. What makes a business idea?

A business idea is a short and precise description of the basic operation of an intended business. Before you start a business, you need to have a clear idea of the sort of business you want to run.

Your business idea will tell you:

- **Which** need will your business fulfill for the customers and what kind of customers will you attract?
- **What** good or service will your business sell?
- **Who** will your business sell to?
- **How** is your business going to sell its goods or services?
- **How much** will your business depend upon and impact the environment? A good business idea will be compatible with the sustainable use of natural resources and will respect the social and natural environment on which it depends.

2.1 Which need will your business fulfill for the customers?

Your business idea should always have customers and their needs in mind.

I wish there was a day care centre near my workplace so that I did not have to spend extra time in taking my son back and forth.

It might be a good idea to start a day care centre in the commercial area as many other parents may have the same need.

It might be a good idea to start a waste collection and recycling service in this area. Not only would the owner of this restaurant need the service, but many other residents in the area might need it as well.

Refer to the cases of Janet and above:

Janet produced sunflower oil without knowing:
- Is there a need for oil?
- Who needs it?
- Why do they need sunflower oil and not another type of cooking oil?

She therefore had no idea how big the demand for sunflower oil would be. Consequently, she could not find customers as the need had been fulfilled by the time she was able to supply her good.

Since Karin did her market research, she knows that pre-teens and teenage girls in her area have limited choice and access to clothing specifically designed for their age group. What they wear is either designed for younger children or for adults. aims to fill the need by producing fashionable clothes that are suitable for their age group.

2.2 What good or service will your business sell?

Depending on your skills and the needs of the customers, you should decide which good or service your business will sell. Also, keep in mind that they must be goods or services that people are willing to pay for and at a price that will allow you to make a profit.

A good is an item that people pay for and use. It may be something you make yourself or it may be something you buy to resell. Tools, baked goods, clothes and retail items are all products .

Making and selling women's clothes

Manufacturing and bottling soya milk for sale

Making and selling household furniture

Making and selling solar lamps

A service is something you do for people that they then pay you for. For example, delivering goods, banking, babysitting, repairing items, collecting recyclable waste from apartment buildings, operating tours, etc. are all services.

Pizza delivery service

Video rental service

Phone repair service

Car wash service

Refer to the cases of Janet and :

Janet grew sunflowers and produced sunflower oil without having any prior knowledge and experience. She was not aware of the challenges of the business, such as the toxics from fertilizers or the long processing time. Janet had no advantage that she could use in her sunflower business and she faced too many problems, so she was unable to make a profit.

Karin had significant experience in making clothes. She knew about sewing. However, she had no experience designing clothes, so she tested her competency by making some designs and showing them to the clothing store owners. She only opened her business after the first batch of dresses were accepted for display in the shops and then sold.

2.3 Who will your business sell to?

Any business cannot succeed without customers. Therefore, it is essential that you know who your customers will be. Will you sell to a specific type of customer or to everyone in an area? There must be enough people who are able and willing to pay for your goods and services or the business will not survive.

Refer to the cases of Janet and Karin:

 Janet had no idea who the end customers of her sunflower oil might be. She just focused on producing the oil and thought that the shops will buy it from her. Therefore, she did not know how big the need was for her good. She also did not know if there were any competitors who were going to fulfil the same needs of the customers.

 Karin knew that her customers will be teenage girls in her area. She researched the market by observing the clothes shops and the target customers to make sure that there was a real need that she could fulfil. She also knew that there was no competitor currently filling that need.

2.4 How is your business going to sell its goods or services?

How are you going to sell your goods or services? If you plan to open a shop, you know how you will sell your product, but manufacturers or service operators can sell their products in many different ways. A manufacturer, for example, can sell either directly to customers, to retailers or to wholesalers.

Some businesses sell directly to their customers:

B&C Furniture makes and sells sofa sets directly to *Melody Café*.

Some businesses sell to retailers:

Jasmine Rice Distributor sells its rice to convenience shops where people go shopping for rice.

Refer to the cases of Janet and Karin:

Janet did not plan how to sell her product. When she made the oil, she just went around and tried to sell to retail shops.

Karin decided from the beginning, to sell her goods through clothes shops. She talked to the owners of these shops even before she started her business, to make sure they would sell her goods.

2.5. How much will your business depend on and impact the environment?

Your business can only be sustainable in the long run if it works in harmony with the social and natural environment. How much does your business depend on the environment? Does it rely on the weather, soil or other natural resources? Does it need any specific type of labour from the local community? Does it need the local community to support it? What should you do to make sure that your business nurtures the natural environment and helps the local community? Will your business nurture the natural environment or will it have a detrimental impact? How would you minimize or reverse any negative effect that your business might have?

The forest is being destroyed by clear cutting. Therefore, wood is becoming scarce and its cost is increasing rapidly. What should I do now to get wood for my business?

Refer to the cases of Janet and Karin:

Janet was not aware of the harmful chemicals in the fertilizers that she uses. Her business will not survive in the long-term if she does not solve the problem of the negative effects of toxic fertilizer. The health of her children will also be adversely affected.

Karin's business addressed a concern of the community-lack of choice and access to appropriate clothing for teenage girls. This is an advantage that her business will use to grow and to stay profitable.

ACTIVITY 3

Now if you already have a business idea, describe your idea using the following form:

My business idea is:
....
....
....

Which need will my business fulfill?
....
....
....

What good/ service will I provide?
....
....
....

To whom will I sell?
....
....
....

How will I sell my good/ service?
....
....
....

How much will my business depend upon and impact the environment?
....
....
....

At this stage, if you cannot adequately describe your idea, it is not a problem. At least you know what information you need for any business idea that you have thought about. You may also need a list of ideas to consider instead of focusing on one vague concept. In the following sections, we will help you find more business ideas before choosing the most suitable one.

PART III

GENERATE SMALL BUSINESS IDEAS LIST

1. Sean's experience

Sean worked for a gas stove importer for five years before he decided to open his own business. His aunt owns a successful hardware supply and rental shop, so she offered to be his financial partner and provide funds for his start-up. She does not want to be involved in the operation, but only to share the profit, while letting Sean run the business himself.

Sean starts thinking about possible business ideas.

He enjoys making sisal bags and wall hangings, which many of his friends admire. Therefore, at first he thinks about making and selling them to tourists as souvenirs. However, after talking to a number of local shopkeepers, he learns that there are too few tourists in his area for such a business to be profitable.

Sean thinks about opening a gas stove shop, as he knows how to source imported gas stoves and he is familiar with the functions and quality of each brand. He does some market research and learns that there are quite a few gas stove shops in his area and their sales are low. They are offering various discount and promotional schemes, but none of their promotions have increased sales significantly. He decides that he better not enter such a tough market.

While still thinking about a business idea, Sean helps his aunt move to a new house. Although it is easy to find a van to rent, no one offers moving services, such as packaging, loading and unloading. Sean has to ask some of his friends to help him package and carry his aunt's furniture and belongings. They spend a whole weekend looking for packaging and then disassembling the big items, wrapping and packing them, loading them in the van, unloading them at the new house and then unpacking and reassembling them. Sean wonders why there is not a moving company in the area. Realizing that this might be a business idea, Sean does some research on that field of business and then describes his business idea as follows:

My business idea: Home/ office packaging and moving service

- **Which need will my business fulfill?** Everyone I talk to agrees that moving from house to house, or office to office is very difficult and time-consuming. There is no company in the area that provides packaging and moving services. Therefore, if I provide these needed services, my business will have a steady demand.

- **What good/service will I provide?** I intend to offer complete packaging and moving services for homes and offices. Although I have no experience running this type of business, I have some experience handling, storing and transporting goods. I learned these things while working with the gas stove importing company. I can ask my brother who is very good at process management to plan the operation. In addition, I can use a reliable transportation provider who often works for my aunt's shop.

- **To whom will I sell?** I intend to start by offering my services to all my relatives, friends, friends of friends and my aunt's customer base. I will then expand my business and advertise around the whole town.

- **How will I sell my service?** I can sell my service directly to the customers. Initially, I will introduce the service to all of my friends, relatives and my aunt's customer base. After I have done some moving for family and friends, I will expand my market and hang posters around areas where there are a lot of shops, offices, apartments and houses for rent.

- **How much will my business depend upon and impact the environment?**
  My business will reuse the cartons and packaging several times so as to prevent waste.

What did Sean do to find his business idea?

_____
_____
_____
_____

Sean does not just focus on one idea:

- He looks around to find different business ideas that may be suitable to his areas of interest and will benefit from his knowledge and his working experience.
- He describes each of the different ideas clearly.
- While researching the different ideas, he found that some would not work because there is not sufficient need, there are not enough customers or the competition is fierce.
- While describing the idea, he also identified resources that he could leverage, such as his friend's knowledge, his aunt's customer base or a reliable transportation provider that he knows.

2. How to identify your own list of business ideas?

Now that you have read about Sean, see if you can find some business ideas for yourself.

Every business idea should be based on knowledge of the market and its needs. The market refers to people who might want to buy a good or service; i.e. the customers. The market differs from place to place, depending on who lives in the area, how they live and for what goods or services they spend their money. When you understand the market in your area, you might recognize many business ideas that you may have previously ignored.

When generating business ideas, it is best to try to keep your mind open to everything. Your first goal is to think of as many ideas as possible and make a list of all the possible business opportunities. With a list, you will have more choices! You then can scan the list and nail down the idea(s) that sound most feasible to you and that you think will be most profitable.

There are many ways to come up with business ideas, such as surveying local businesses or asking existing business owners. Below, we will examine a few different approaches to generating business ideas. The information gained from one approach may supplement another and help you to clearly describe your business ideas. Write down your business ideas on an idea list using the different approaches to find new ideas (see the following example).

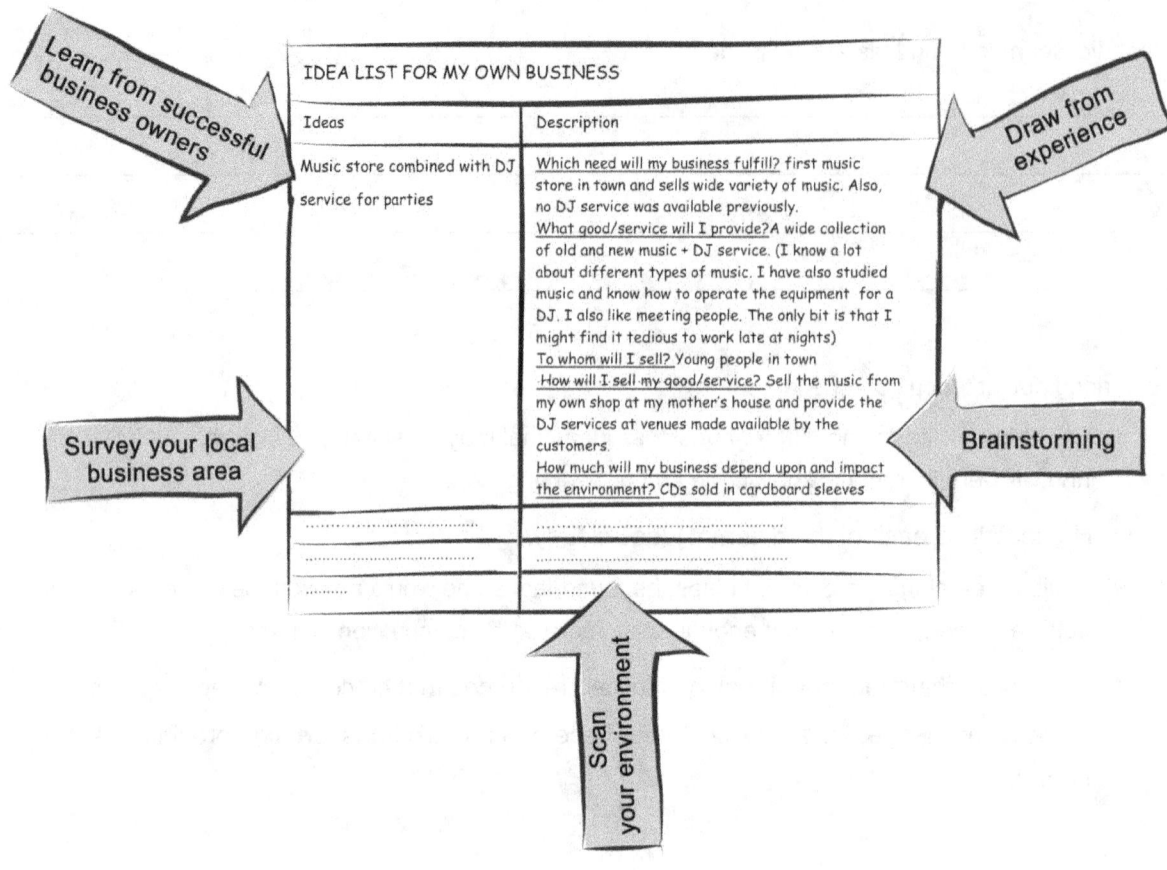

Each approach (represented by the arrows in the example above) will be discussed in the next sections.

3. Learn from successful business owners

You can learn a lot from people in your area who have already gone through the process of establishing a business. You should try to get the following information from them:

- What kind of idea did these businesses start with?
- Where did the ideas come from?
- How did they develop their ideas into successful businesses?
- How does the business profit and fit into the local environment?
- Where did they get the money to start their business?

Muthoni is looking for an idea to start her own business. She decided to talk to successful business people in her area. Muthoni phoned Sean and made an appointment to see him. When she went to meet Sean she used the Business Ideas Analysis Form shown below, to write down his answers to her questions.

BUSINESS IDEAS ANALYSIS FORM

Name of business: *Sean Packaging and Moving*

Goods or services sold: A full package of home and office moving services

Main customers: Individuals and businesses who need to change their home or office location

When and why did the owner decide to start this business?

Sean started his business in 2009 when he needed to earn extra income. While helping his aunt move to a new house, he found that moving was a very big job and that there was no packaging and moving company in his area. Also, he had some experience in handling, storing and transporting goods that he had gained while working with a gas stove importing company.

Why did the owner think it was a good idea to start that kind of business?

Sean did some market research and learned that a considerable number of people in his area move their homes and offices frequently. They all complain that moving is a formidable task and that there is no packaging and moving service in town to assist them.

How did the owner find out what his potential customers wanted?

Sean talked to lots of friends, relatives, owners of businesses and neighbours.

What strengths or assets did the owner use to start this business?

(E.g., previous experience, training, social networks, contacts, hobbies) Sean had an aunt who was in business and was willing to assist him to finance his business. He had gained experience in packing, storing and transporting goods in his previous job. He also had a brother who helped him organize the operation.

What problems did the owner face while setting up the business?

Sean did not know much about marketing, so it was initially difficult for him to get the word out about his unique service.

Has the business good or service changed over time?

The business has expanded. He now has his own van and is planning to buy two more vans and to employ more staff next year.

What is the impact of the business on the natural environment and the community?

Sean reuses the packaging cartons and materials at least two or three times before selling them to his local recycling centre. Therefore, he not only saves costs but also reduces waste. (People who do their own packaging and moving often throw away the packaging materials afterwards.) His business provides employment to people in his community. People with lower education are also able to get a job in his business as he assigns basic tasks to them.

Notes:

- Sometimes what you enjoy doing may not translate into a profitable business idea. Sean would not have been able to make a profit from selling sisal bags.
- The first idea may not always the best one. It is important to get factual information about the market before acting on the idea. Sean found out about the lack of a market for his bags before he started the business.
- If you find a good idea but lack sufficient training in some aspects, you can employ qualified staff or establish business links.
- It may be necessary to source financial help before you can start a business.
- Sean's business idea was successful because it was based on an obvious business opportunity and knowledge of the market.

 ## ACTIVITY 4

Now find out about some successful business ideas in your area.

- Think of three businesses in your local area that you consider to be successful. Try to select businesses that are at least three years old. In the space below, write the name of each business and the goods or services it sells.

_____
_____
_____
_____
_____
_____

- Make three forms like the one on page 30 for each of the three businesses listed above.
- Go and talk to the owners of those three businesses. See if they agree with you that their businesses are successful. Ask them how they decided to go into that business. Did they see a need in the market that was not being met? Did they have some experience, contacts or skills to build upon? Did they know someone else in the business? Was this the first business they ever worked in? Write down any other questions that you want to ask the owners, in the space on the next page.

_____
_____
_____
_____
_____
_____
_____
_____
_____
_____
_____

- • After you finish talking to the owners, complete a Business Ideas Analysis Form for each business, listing as many details as possible.

- • Think about all the factors that have made the business idea a good one and why it has become a successful business. Find answers to the following questions and write them on the form under "Notes":

    — What lessons can you draw from the experiences of the business owner?

    — What mistakes do you think the owner made?

    — How can you avoid the same mistakes?

    — What do you think has made the business a success?

When you have completed the activity you will have a better understanding of how business ideas are created. You will also be aware of the problems people have when they try to find a business idea and turn it into a real business.

BUSINESS IDEAS ANALYSIS FORM

Name of business: _____

Goods or services sold: _____

Main customers: _____

When and why did the owner decide to start this business?
_____
_____

Why did the owner think it was a good idea to start that kind of business?
_____
_____

How did the owner learn what his potential customers wanted?
_____
_____

What strengths or assets did the owner use to start this business? (E.g., previous experience, training, family background, contacts, hobbies)
_____
_____

What problems did the owner face in setting up the business?
_____
_____

Has the business good or service changed over time?
_____
_____

What is the impact of the business on the natural environment and the community?
_____
_____

Notes:

_____
_____

4. Draw from experience

4.1 Your own experience

Look at the list of your interests, your experiences and your networks on page 7 (Part I, section 2.3). Are there any possible business ideas that you can derive from your own past experience? Think about each type of experience.

Start with yourself. What has your experience been as a customer in the market place? Have you ever searched all day for some items that you could not find in any store in your area? Think about the goods and services you have wanted at different times and that you have had difficulty finding.

4.2 Other people's experiences

The people around you are potential customers. It is important to understand their experience trying to find goods and services that are unavailable or not exactly what they need. Listen carefully to what these people say about their shopping experience.

Ask your family and friends about the things they would like to find that are not locally available. Expand your social knowledge by talking to people from different age groups, social classes, etc. You can also visit community groups, colleges, etc. for a greater understanding of the market.

Here are some examples of comments that would help with your search for a business idea:

- "I cannot find a lunch box that keeps the food warm."
- "The choice of cooking pots in the shops is very limited."
- "There is no reliable way of sending gift packages to my friends and relatives living in the villages."
- "There is not enough entertainment in this town and the weekends are so boring."
- "I really need to buy some marketing textbooks, but there are no good bookstores in this town."
- "There is so much garbage on the streets. Somebody should do something about it."
- "I cannot find a decent house painter in this town. The ones I have hired do not prepare the surface properly before painting and they paint over everything including the dirt."
- "There is only one garment shop in town. But the sales lady is so rude. She also seems disinterested in showing the clothes to the customers."
- "The local hospital does not have a drug store close to it. I have to take the bus to the nearest store to get the medicines prescribed by the doctor."
- "I do not like the way the local grocery shopkeeper treats his employees, but there is no other place near here where I can find the things I need."
- "There is no canteen or café near the factory and it is hard to get a snack or a cup of tea when I want it."
- "Whenever a machine breaks down, it is difficult to get it serviced quickly."
- "Fertilizers from the market are way too expensive and there is no organic alternative."

Complete Activity 5 below and think of the possible business ideas you can derive from the experiences you list.

ACTIVITY 5

Note your experiences as a customer or what other people have said about their experiences as customers in the space below. Then write down the related business idea that would provide customers with the goods or services they need and want.

Personal experience	Business ideas
Other people's experiences as customers	Business ideas
Comments about poor service	Business ideas
Difficulties encountered while trying to accomplish something	Business ideas
Environmental problems	Business ideas

Add these business ideas to your idea list (use the form on page 47). Try to describe each idea as clearly as possible, based on the following five criteria:
- •• Which need will my business fulfill?
- •• What good/ service will I provide?
- •• To whom will I sell?
- •• How will I sell my good/service?
- •• How much will my business depend upon and impact the environment?

5. Survey your local business area

Another way of discovering business ideas is to look around your local community. Find out what type of businesses are already operating in your area and see if you can identify any gaps in the market.

If you live in a village or small town, you may be able to identify all the fields of business in the whole town. Otherwise, you may need to focus on the preferred business fields and business types that you identified in Part I of the guidebook. This is an activity that will be much easier to do with a business partner or friend. Visit the closest industrial area, markets and shopping centres in your area.

Muthoni's experience

Muthoni is trying to think of business ideas. She collects information about the businesses operating in the town where she lives so that she can get ideas to start her own business. Muthoni likes cooking. She was working part-time in a bakery when she was in her college. She is also interested in home decoration and fashion. Muthoni likes meeting different people. Therefore, she prefers to open a service or retail business related to cooking, home décor or fashion.

What Muthoni does:

- Visits the local shopping mall where there are a lot of high-end restaurants, garment stores and household goods
- Walks around the local central market, where people often go to shop for furniture, garments, appliances and household decorations at reasonable rates
- Visits the commercial district where a lot of wholesalers for food and clothing operate. It is also the hub of hardware products
- Talks to the local business association about the kinds of businesses registered with it and also checks the yellow pages for additional businesses being advertised

Muthoni is interested in cooking, home décor and fashion. Therefore, she prepares a list of all businesses related to it that exist in the area she inspected.

Cooking related	Home décor related	Fashion related
— 5 bakeries	— 1 furniture factory producing wooden furniture	— 12 tailors
— 12 food stores	— 3 furniture shops	— 5 clothing shops for ladies
— 3 restaurants	— 1 handmade home décor shop	— 2 maternity shops
— 5 cafés	— 2 small galleries	— 7 shoe and handbag shops
— 8 street food stalls	— 4 interior decoration shops selling lamps, paints, wallpaper, art frames, décor items	— 4 clothing shops for children
— 6 shops selling drinks		— 2 men's clothing shops
— 2 catering services that provide their services at the customers' venues	— 3 gift shops	— 2 traditional clothing shops

Muthoni also makes the following general observations about her town:

- Majority of the local people do not have a lot of cash. They mostly shop at small inexpensive kiosks and there are no luxury or leisure shops.
- Farming is the main economic activity in the area.
- It is a local tourist spot and a lot of people from the neighbouring towns visit it. There are a plenty of small hotels and bars.
- The number of young people seems to be increasing. There are many nursery schools.
- This is evidently a growing and thriving town as there are a number of building contractors and construction supply stores.
- The environmental situation is deteriorating. Neither business owners nor the local residents are concerned about pollution. There is garbage on the streets and the local factories are polluting the air.

Muthoni then makes the following list of businesses that do not operate in her town which might be good business opportunities. To produce this list, she thinks about the nearby towns that she has visited and notes the goods and services that are available in those towns, but not available in her area.

Cooking related	**Home décor related**	**Fashion related**
— Fresh meal shop for babies — Cooking class for visitors — Catering service providing inexpensive lunch boxes to offices — Shops for teenagers offering soft drinks, bubble teas, milk shakes, fresh fruit drinks and ice-cream outside universities and schools	— Art frames and shelves made to order (service) — Convenient home storage products (retailer) — Handmade home décor items from recycled materials (manufacturer) — Home décor picture gallery with café (service) — Plastic/ paper flowers for home decoration (retailer)	— Tailor making and selling fashionable clothing — Second-hand clothes shop. — Basic sewing training for teenagers — Handmade home decorations made from recycled clothing

By matching each idea against a possible need for the people in her town, Muthoni is able to focus on a few of these ideas, including:

- Fresh meal shop for babies
- Catering service delivering lunches to offices
- Shop and refreshment stand for teenagers
- Home décor picture gallery with café
- Store selling plastic and paper flowers for home decoration
- Secondhand clothing store
- Handmade decorative items made from recycled clothing

Muthoni also searches on the internet and reads business publications for more ideas.

 *Learn more about discovering business ideas in the next section – Scanning the environment.*

ACTIVITY 6

Follow the steps below to collect information about existing businesses and potential new businesses in your local area or in the location where you want to start your own business.

1. Revisit the assessment on page 7 (Part I, section 2.3) for the business field in which you are most interested.

2. Use the form below to write down the different business options that are available in your local area and that are within your field interest.

Business field............	Business field............	Business field............

3. Study the list and try to find answers to the following questions:

   •• In which businesses are there many potential competitors? In which are there only a few? Can you think why there are so many businesses in this field?

   •• What does your list tell you about your local market and the way people spend money in your area? Write down at least five observations about your local market.

4. Is there room for another business in the field that is of interest to you? Do you think there is a business opportunity for you?

   •• Write down in the box below some businesses that do not exist in your area.

   •• Possible businesses in your area:

Business field............	Business field............	Business field............

You can also amend this list after studying the next section: "Scanning your environment".

6. Scanning your environment

You can use your creativity to find more business ideas in your area. Look at the list of existing local businesses. If the list has included most of the local markets, you may be able to learn about the industries or service providers on which the local economy relies.

Muthoni's town is a farming centre, which depends on agriculture. It provides services to many surrounding small villages. Maybe your town depends on mining, fishing, industry or tourism. Maybe there are a number of educational or publicly funded institutions that employ many people in your area.

It may be useful to think about business ideas by considering all the resources and institutions in your area. For example think about:

- Natural resources
- Characteristics and skills of people in the local community
- Import substitution
- Waste products
- Publications
- Trade fairs and exhibitions

6.1 Natural resources

Think of what is abundantly available in your area that could be made into useful products without harming the environment. Natural resources include materials from soil, agriculture, forest, mineral, water, etc.

Perhaps there is good clay soil in the area that can be used for making bricks. It may be used for other business ventures such as making plates, cups or tiles.

Think about a way to use this resource that would enable you to continue working with it for many years. In other words, make sure that your business idea will not exhaust the natural resource that would be the foundation of your business.

6.2 Characteristics and skills of people in the local community

Consider whether the people in your area have some special characteristics or skills that could be useful for a business:

- Are there people in your community who are good artisans, tailors or carpenters or who have specific skills creating items unique to your area?
- Are there recent graduates looking for jobs who you could employ?
- Are there caregivers, nurses or people who could offer services to children, the elderly or the sick?
- Is your community digitally connected?
- Is the infrastructure in your community well developed?
- ...

6.3 Waste products

Business opportunities can also be generated by using materials that have been previously used by both homeowners and businesses. Think about the possible use of waste materials for the production of other useful and marketable items. Recyclable waste products can be identified by analysing certain items to see how they are discarded. Man-made waste has a detrimental effect on the environment. In most cases, companies are keen to work with entrepreneurs who can turn their waste products into valuable and marketable items.

Usually there is something that can be reused in things that we throw away. Recycling may be done with waste products that come from agricultural processing, household garbage, used machinery and appliances or industrial waste. People throw out food that could be used to make compost or animal feed. They also throw away paper, glass and aluminium that can be recycled. Think of things that can be made from what others thought was garbage.

Many industries dispose of useful materials. A clothing company might throw out small pieces of cloth that could be used to make something else. Plastics factories usually have materials left over that might be useful for insulation, stuffing for pillows or a new kind of fuel.

Is there a possibility that you could recycle something that is found in abundance in your neighbourhood? Is there a way of using resources more efficiently? Maybe you could offer a service to help individuals or institutions dispose of their waste in a way that is environmentally-friendly or maybe you can make something new out of the waste.

6.4 Import substitution

Can you think of anything that is imported that might be made locally? Some imported goods have high import duties, making them very expensive. You could investigate the possibility of operating a business that can easily make the imported goods locally.

6.5 Publications

Publications from the internet and other printed material may help you find ideas. There are many sites on the internet that you can visit to find out about business ideas as well as franchise businesses for sale. There are also web-based businesses that you can search from home if you have internet connection.

Newspapers are a great source of ideas. They often describe types of businesses that you could start or products that you could provide in your area. The classified advertisements may give you ideas, as well as articles about business trends in other places.

6.6 Trade fairs and exhibitions

Organizations hold trade fairs for different goods or services. Attending these fairs may give you exposure to a number of new business ideas that you had not previously considered. Be sure to attend any trade fair for fields of business in which you may be interested.

 ACTIVITY 7

Take time to look around your own community and make notes for each of the following:

Natural resources	Business ideas
Waste products	Business ideas
Import substitution	Business ideas
Publications	Business ideas
Trade fairs and exhibitions	Business ideas

Add these business ideas to your idea list (use the form on page 47). Try to describe each idea as clear as possible based on the following five criteria:
- Which need will my business fulfill?
- What good/ service will I provide?
- To whom will I sell?
- How will I sell my good/service?
- How much will my business depend upon and impact the environment?

7. Brainstorming

Brainstorming means opening up your mind and thinking about many different ideas. You start with a word or a topic and then write down everything that comes to mind relating to that subject. You continue writing for as long as possible, putting down things that you think of, even if they seem irrelevant or odd. Good ideas can come from concepts that initially seem strange.

Brainstorming works best in a group. Get your family or friends together and ask them to help by writing down ideas they have when they hear the word or subject matter.

We will use Ken as an example. He asked his sister and two friends to brainstorm with him to find a business idea. He has worked as a carpenter in a furniture factory for a long time so they started with the word "wood". At first the ideas for businesses related to wood came slowly. But soon they had many possibilities.

ACTIVITY 8

Do some brainstorming yourself.

1. Start with a word related to a type and field of business in which you are interested or that you know about and write down all the ideas that pop into your mind. Continue until you cannot think of anything else.

_____

_____

_____

_____

2. Now go back and check the words you have written. Do the words give you ideas for a business that you can imagine starting?

_____

_____

Even if you cannot find any ideas you like, the exercise is useful for helping you to open your mind to a new way of thinking. Now pick another word based on your skills, past work experience, academic background or interests and write down all the products related to that word on a new piece of paper.

The more often you brainstorm the better you will get at coming up with feasible business ideas.

8. Structured brainstorming

Structured brainstorming is when you think of the different processes that are involved in the operation of a particular business and the goods/services that can be offered with respect to those processes. This is differ-ent from thinking about random items related to a particular business field and type.

Try to think of all the businesses that are related to different aspects of a product:

- • Those involved in production
- • Those involved in the selling process
- • Those involved in recycling or re-using materials
- • Those indirectly related (spin-offs)
- • Those involved in servicing

This can be illustrated as follows:

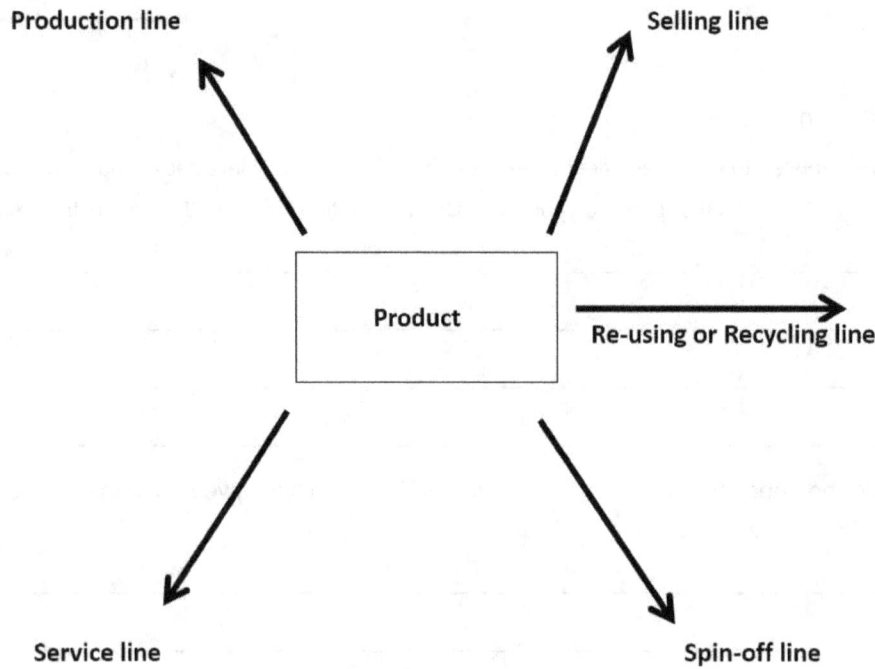

You can think of different processes within each line. You continue until you have run out of ideas. Again, what-ever comes to mind should be written down. Decide later if it is worthwhile or correct. Let's take the example of cotton T-shirts:

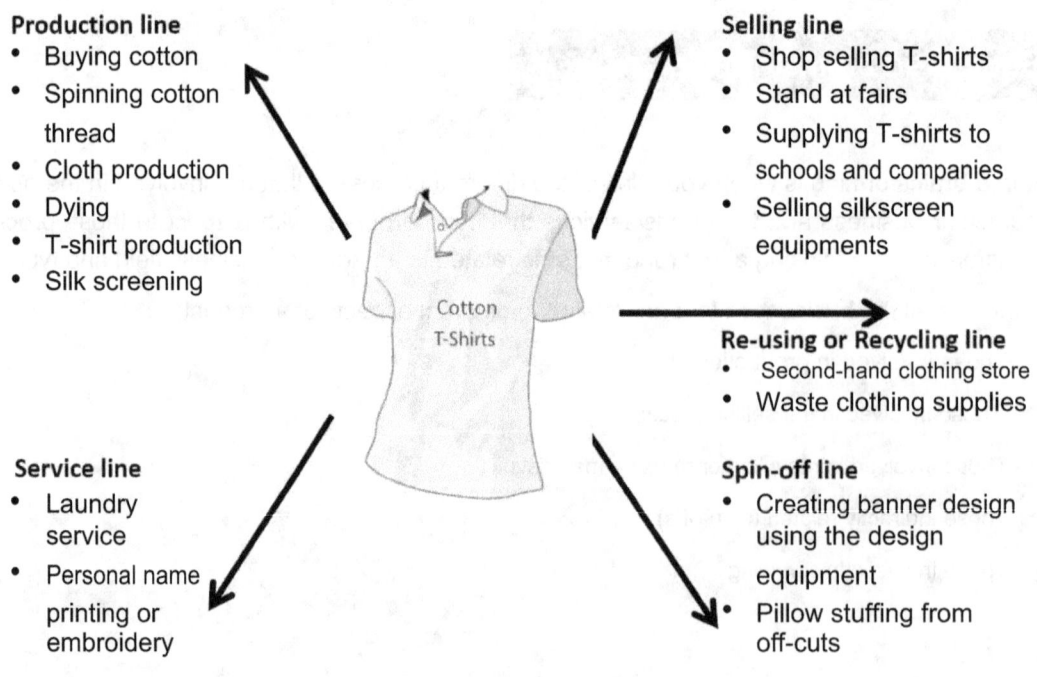

ACTIVITY 9

Try some structured brainstorming by yourself.

Pick a product you know something about. It can be from your training, your experience or your interests. It may be an idea you already have for your own business or you may choose one of the products you learned about when you spoke to the owners of successful businesses in your area.

Use the diagram in the space below. Write the product and related business field in the central box.

Then start brainstorming for each production line, selling line, re-using or recycling line, spin-off line and service line.

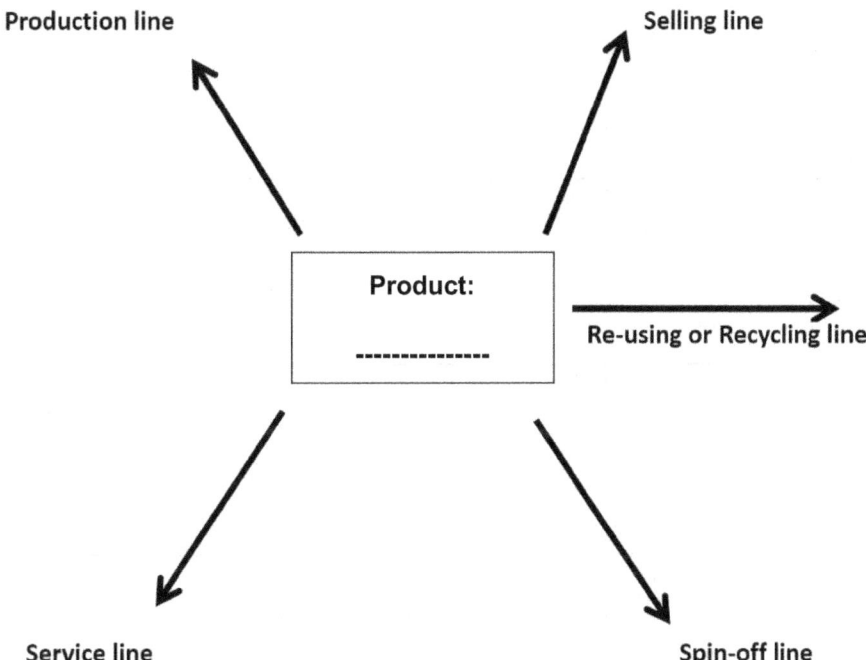

You can do this exercise as many times as you want to, using a different product each time. Use a new piece of paper and diagram for each product.

If you do not yet have many business ideas on your ideas list, repeat all the techniques you have used so far, as you learn more about the market and more about business.

Remember that a successful business is always based on a good business idea. If you have a list of ideas, you will have more choices to consider and more opportunities to choose a good business idea. It is worth taking the time and making the effort to really work hard at identifying ideas that are suitable and appropriate.

9. Your ideas list

ACTIVITY 10

Now consider all the activities you have done in this section when filling in the idea list below:

MY IDEAS LIST	
Ideas	Description

PART IV

THE BEST BUSINESS IDEAS FOR YOU

1. Screen your ideas list

After doing all of the things described in Part III, Muthoni came up with 17 business ideas. However, when considering the following five criteria, her list has been reduced to only six ideas.

- Which need is to be fulfilled?
- What good or service will the business sell?
- Who will the business sell to?
- How will the business sell its good or service?
- How much will the business depend upon and impact the environment?

These six on her short list are now the best ideas that she will consider.

MY IDEAS LIST	
Ideas	**Description**
Solar lamps and chargers	**Which need is to be fulfilled?** Need for lighting in areas where the electricity is unreliable, expensive and the power is often cut. **What good/service?** Solar lamps and chargers. There is an NGO currently teaching people how to make solar lighting and chargers. There is also a programme for financing businesses that produce solar products. **Who to sell to?** All the homes and businesses in my area, as the power here is often cut off. **How to sell?** Through hardware stores. **How will the environment be affected?** The lamp uses solar energy, a form of renewable energy. The charger will be durable so that it has a long life and does not need to be replaced often. Dumping of chargers that have toxic chemicals inside will be done in such a way that does not pollute the environment or seep into the water table.

	A catering service delivering lunches to offices	**Which need is to be fulfilled?** People in offices need fresh food at a reasonable price delivered to them during lunch time. No one else in town does this. **What good/ service?** Delivery of lunch boxes. I know how to cook and I enjoy it. Not much money is needed to start. **Who to sell to?** Office workers in the city centre. **How to sell?** By providing a phone number for people to call in the morning and order one of the four lunch sets available every day. **How will the environment be affected?** Disposable styrofoam containers are difficult to eliminate and are not environmentally-friendly. Paper is better, but it still requires wood from trees, which contributes to degradation of the forests. I would rather use reusable containers; however it is a bit difficult to collect them after lunch every day.
	A tile-making business	**Which need is to be fulfilled?** A lot of people in this town are building houses and need tiles. There is no other business manufacturing tiles in this town, so all the retailers buy from a tile factory in another area. **What good/service?** Tiles. The local clay is good for making tiles and, is plentiful and cheap. I do not know how to make tiles but they are beautiful and I would enjoy learning. The equipment would be expensive. **Who to sell to?** Retailers in the area who are buying tiles from the factories in other localities. But the problem is that I am not sure how many customers there will be or if I could make tiles that are as high quality as those produced in the factories. **How to sell?** Through the construction material retailers in the area. **How will the environment be affected?** Making clay tiles is not harmful to the environment.
	Second-hand clothing store	**Which need is to be fulfilled?** There are lots of people who want nice clothing but cannot afford to buy new clothes. **What good/service?** A second-hand clothing store. There is no similar shop in town. I would be careful to buy used clothing that is fashionable and sell it at a price well below the prices in the local clothing stores. I once worked in a clothing store. I have a good eye for fashion and I know how to recognize good quality clothes. I would really enjoy running a shop, meeting people and selling fashionable clothing. **Who to sell to?** Low income families and students on a tight budget. **How to sell?** I will rent a shop space in the centre of town. I need to find out how much it will cost to rent a space. **How will the environment be affected?** This is a business that recycles clothing, so it is good for the environment. My business relies on a good supply of second-hand clothes.

	Agency for home-based care	**Which need is to be fulfilled?** There is a need for home-based hospice or medical care, as the local hospitals are very busy and do not provide hospice care for terminally ill patients. There is no business like this in this town. The community really needs this type of service as a lot of people have to work and have no time to look after their sick relatives. **What good/ service?** A service that provides home-based care. I have often looked after sick people. Also, my sister is a nurse and she could help me. I could get into a medical aid scheme or work with a donor financed NGO to source financing to care for those who are unable to pay for the service. Many women in my community could be employed to provide this service. I would enjoy this work as I like to help other people. **Who to sell to?** Families with elderly and/or sick people. **How to sell?** I would open an agency office and advertise my service in local newspapers, on the internet and through the local doctors and hospitals. **How will environment be affected?** The community would welcome this service as it is an ethical business that helps those in need.
	Garbage collection	**Which need is to be fulfilled?** Many people complain that they do not know where to dump their garbage and that the municipal government does not provide a regular, frequent collection service. It also does not have a landfill site that is open to the public so that people can dispose of their trash. **What good/ service?** A garbage collection service. Besides providing a badly needed service and collecting money for it, there is additional revenue that can be made from recycling products such as plastics, metals, paper and textiles. Perhaps the municipal government would give me a contract. A friend used to work in the department responsible for garbage collection so he could advise me. **Who to sell to?** We would be providing a community service, so there should be lots of customers willing to pay something to get rid of the garbage. Once we have a landfill site and have purchased trucks to pick up garbage, we would set up accounts for every home and business in the area and connect with companies that recycle waste to buy the recyclable materials from us. **How to sell?** Direct collection. Start-up capital for vehicles and drivers would be needed. There is however, a push cart that the local environmental conservation NGO has been promoting that can be used for collecting household garbage. I could also start small by using the push cart and working with a team of unemployed youth in the community to start providing the service and then expand the business as money comes in to buy garbage collection trucks. **How will the environment be affected?** This service helps clean up the environment.

You may already have your own idea list. Although each of your business ideas has been described, there is probably still a lot you do not know about the businesses on the list. The questions below will help you to continue to get more information and to make a shorter list with the three best ideas.

Try to answer these questions for each idea:

WHICH

- Which unfulfilled need do you want to satisfy for your customers?
- Which needs do your goods or services satisfy for the customers?

WHAT

- What goods or services do your customers want?
- What quality of products do your customers want?
- What information do you have about the goods or services for this business?
- What are the positive or negative impacts your business will have on your community and the natural environment?

WHO

- Who will be your customers for this particular business? Will there be enough of them to make your business profitable?
- Who are your competitors and what are their strengths and weaknesses?

HOW

- How will you be able to supply the quality of goods and services that your customers want?
- How much do you know about the quality of goods and services that your customers want?
- How does running this sort of business suit your personal characteristics, skills and situation?
- How do you know that there is a need for this business in your area?
- How do you think you will feel about running this business in ten years?

OTHER IMPORTANT QUESTIONS TO CONSIDER

- Where can you get advice and information about this business?
- Will this be the only business of this type in your area?
- If there are other similar businesses, how will you be able to successfully compete with them?
- What is your competitive advantage? (For example, would you be providing more efficient goods and services that would eventually replace those that exist at the moment? Would your business eventually show higher growth rates than existing businesses as a result of the advantages?)
- Why do you think this business will be viable?

- Does this business need equipment, premises or qualified staff? Do you think you will be able to get the finances to provide these things?
- Where will you get the resources to start this business?
- Could your business model save money by reducing, re-using or recycling?

To answer these questions objectively, you should get more information by doing a field study.

2. Field study

By talking to possible future customers or suppliers and to members of the business community, you can gather useful information about the factors that would affect your business idea. You could just have informal discussions and make observations or you could arrange more formal visits and interviews. The visits will take time and effort, but by doing field research, you would already be starting to act like a successful businessperson. The contacts you make during these visits would also be useful when you start your business.

2.1 Conducting your interviews

Collecting information for your business gives you an opportunity to promote your business idea and to present yourself as a potential entrepreneur. Describe your idea positively and explain why you think it will be something customers want. Talk about how your idea will contribute positively to the development of your community. Ask open-ended questions using the "who", "what", "why", "where", "when", "how" methodology of getting more information. Let the conversation flow naturally.

2.2 Who to talk to?

There are three important groups that you should talk to:

- Potential customers: Their views are essential to your understanding of whether or not your proposed product is important to them and if you need to modify your idea to meet their needs.
- Competitors, suppliers and entities with financial resources: Their views will reveal the challenges of competition that you would face, as well as other issues related to your potential business.
- Financial institutions: Find out the lending requirements to determine whether borrowing for a new business is possible.
- Key informants and opinion leaders: These are people who would know a lot about the type and field of business you want to go into and/or a lot about your potential customers. Their views would give you a lot to think about and could also give you a better insight into the feasibility of your business idea.

ACTIVITY 11

For each business idea, plan how to get more information through field study by completing the form below:

Business idea:	
What do I need to find out?	
Who will I talk to?	**What questions to ask?**
1...............	
2...............	
3...............	
4...............	

After you have acquired more information for each business idea, you will notice several reasons why some ideas are stronger than the others. For example, an idea may be received well by potential customers and may have very little competition in the marketplace, but may need a huge initial capital investment. On the other hand, there might be a business idea that is popular with potential customers, but that has some competition and needs less initial investment. Therefore, the second idea might be more feasible if you do not have access to a large amount of money.

Make note of the three ideas that meet all the criteria and would offer the best potential. Once you have reduced your list of business ideas to the three that are most suitable, the next step is to use a SWOT analysis tool to select the best idea out of the three.

3. SWOT analysis

One method people often use to decide the most suitable business idea is a SWOT analysis. It helps you to focus on the possible problem areas and the potential advantages of each idea.

SWOT stands for:
- **S** Strengths
- **W** Weaknesses
- **O** Opportunities
- **T** Threats

3.1 Inside the business

To analyse the strengths and weaknesses of your business idea, evaluate what will the business be good at and what the potential drawbacks or problems might be.

Strengths are the specific positive aspects which will give your proposed business an advantage over similar business ventures and the competitors. It could be that you propose to sell a better quality product or that you have a location which is more accessible to your customers. There will always be demand for new products that offer new ways of solving old problems or are more efficient than other products. Could your good or service benefit from having a Fair Trade or Organic Product certificate? Customers are inclined to pay higher prices for Fair Trade or Organic Products.

Weaknesses are the things that your business will not do as well as other businesses. Perhaps your costs will be higher because your business is located a long way from the source of supplies needed for production and you will have to pay more for transport or perhaps you are unable to meet the quality standards of the competition.

3.2 Outside the business

To analyse the opportunities and threats of your proposed business, look at the external environment. What aspects of the environment will benefit the business and what aspects will negatively affect the business?

Opportunities are on-going potential developments that will be good for your business. It could be that the demand for the product you are proposing will increase because of an influx of tourists. It could also be that new regulations enacted by the government for the promotion of green jobs and social enterprises will result in a higher demand for the type of products that you will provide.

Threats are events that may negatively affect your business. For example, the business idea could be so simple that other people may start similar businesses in your area and reduce your share of the market. There could also be proposed legislation affecting the operation of your business, such as restrictions on the import of certain products.

Once you have identified your SWOT, try matching your Strengths and Opportunities to ascertain whether or not they will give your business an advantage. For example, if people are looking for a service that matches your proposed product (Opportunities) and you are very service oriented and care about details (Strengths), you may be creating a big advantage for your proposed business.

You may also match your Weaknesses and Threats to determine if you can improve your weak points to cope with the threats. On the other hand, if the two present a major obstacle to the potential for profit, you may consider deleting that business idea.

Based on the information collected from her field study, Muthoni has chosen the three most suitable ideas:

- Agency for home-based care
- Catering service delivering lunch boxes to offices
- Second-hand clothing store

The table on the next page shows how Muthoni does the SWOT analysis for one of her proposed businesses: A store selling second-hand clothes to people in the local community.

SWOT ANALYSIS	
Business idea: Second-hand clothing store	
STRENGTHS I have some work experience in clothing stores. I love fashion. I can recognize good quality clothing. I enjoy meeting people. I am good at making attractive displays.	**WEAKNESSES** I do not have an available spot for the business (I must rent a shop). I do not have many sources of cheap second-hand clothing. I have no experience managing staff. I have no experience controlling stock.
OPPORTUNITIES There is no other second-hand shop in the town. New clothes are expensive and there are not many with good designs. There is a huge customer base among students and the lower middle class. Majority of the local people do not have a lot of cash to spare in one go. People tend to save money on clothes when they have less money to spare. There is a growing trend of recycling to be environmental friendly.	**THREATS** People tend to use their clothes longer in this type of economy and do not throw them away. The business is easily copied. I might lose my market share if other stores open in the area. The cost of renting the shop space is high. Loss from theft is a major problem in our community.

Advantages:

- There is a huge customer base among students and the lower middle class. People do not want to spend a lot of money on clothes, but still they do desire beautiful and good quality clothing. I am capable of choosing second-hand clothes that meet these requirements.
- I am good at fashion and decoration, so I can make the shop look attractive with fashionable clothes. People will be happy to find unique clothing at reasonable prices.
- The business matches the growing trend of recycling to be environmental friendly.

Disadvantages:

- Without multiple sources of second-hand clothing, it will be difficult for me to choose the best clothes for my shop. I must source more used clothing in larger cities and think about asking my friends to collect used clothing from their network of friends, relatives and colleagues.
- All costs are increasing, so I may not make much of a profit if I'm not careful. I must control the stock and price the clothing with enough of a margin to cover my increased costs. I should either register for a stock control training course or ask a friend who knows about stock control to teach me.
- I must always improve my good and service to stay ahead of the competition.

Muthoni also does a SWOT for each of the other two business ideas and compares all the advantages and disadvantages of the three.

Second-hand clothing store	Catering service delivering lunch boxes to offices	Agency for home-based care
Advantages: — There is a huge customer base among students and the lower middle class with an increasing trend towards shopping for less expensive items. However, they still want fashionable, quality clothing. I am capable of choosing second-hand clothes that meet these requirements. — I am good at fashion and decoration, so I can make the shop look attractive with displays of fashionable clothes. People will be happy to find quality clothing at reasonable prices. — The business matches the growing trend of recycling to be environmental friendly.	**Advantages:** — Working professionals have very little time to make lunch before they go to work. Also, very few work places have good canteens. There will be a strong demand for my business. — I am a good cook. I will provide lunches with different options every day. Even if competition develops, I should not lose customers. — People always want good quality products at a reasonable price. My price will be competitive because I will not have to rent a food shop. I also have some relatives who can supply fresh food at a discounted price.	**Advantages:** — The demand for this service has risen significantly due to the increased lifespan and the subsequent growing number of senior citizens, many of whom need constant medical care. I have a good network of housewives who would like to earn some money. — My sister and I can train these women in basic care for the sick and elderly. — People are concerned about trusting caregivers with their loved ones when they are not at home or out working. I know these women and their relatives, so I can vouch for them.
Disadvantages: — Without multiple sources of second-hand clothing, it will be difficult to choose the best clothes for my shop. I must source more used clothing in larger cities and think about asking my friends to collect used clothing from their network of friends, relatives and colleagues. — All costs are increasing, so I may not make much of a profit if I'm not careful. I must control the stock and price the clothing with enough of a margin to cover my increased costs. I should either register for a stock control training course or ask a friend who knows about stock control to teach me. — I must always improve my good and service to stay ahead of the competition.	**Disadvantages:** — This business will involve quite a number of staff but I do not have experience managing people. I must learn about business operation and personnel management. — There may be people who copy my business idea, especially people who have food stalls near the office complexes. It may take them less time to deliver to the offices. They also have more experience.	**Disadvantages:** — There may be serious risks related to the health of the clients. My staff can only handle simple cases. I need to create an SOS process and make my responsibilities clear in the contract with clients.

By making this comparison, Muthoni thinks that all three have advantages but that she would be best suited to manage the disadvantages of the second-hand clothing store. She also thinks that she is more interested in that idea, as it fits well with her love of fashion. She decides to choose the second-hand clothing store as her business.

ACTIVITY 12

Now do a SWOT analysis for each of the three business ideas you have selected.

First make three copies of the SWOT analysis form as shown on the next page and then write down the first of your three selected business ideas on the first form.

Think carefully about the strengths and weaknesses within the business. These may be personal characteristics, financial issues, marketing issues, the location of the business or the cost of promoting and selling your product. Write all of them down.

Think of the external environment for this business. What are the opportunities and threats in your business environment? The "key informants" you spoke to during your field research may have pointed these out to you. Write them down.

Ask yourself:

- Can I combine my strengths with the opportunities to create a big advantage?
- What disadvantages are created by the weaknesses and the threats? Can I overcome them? How?

Then write down the advantages and disadvantages, as well as how you intend to overcome them.

When you are finished with your first idea, use the two copies of the form to do the same SWOT analysis for your next two ideas.

SWOT ANALYSIS	
Business idea:	
STRENGTHS	WEAKNESSES
OPPORTUNITIES	THREATS

Advantages:

Disadvantages:

When you have completed the three SWOT analyses for the three business ideas, compare them and select the business which has more advantages and less disadvantages and /or is easier to overcome the disadvantages.

PART V

GENERATE SMALL BUSINESS IDEAS

If you have decided on the right idea, congratulations!

ACTIVITY 13

Now you can complete a summary of your business idea in the box below.

My business idea: ....

Type of business: ☐ Manufacturing ☐ Service provision
☐ Wholesaling ☐ Retailing

Field of business: ....

My goods or services will be: ....
....

My customers will be: ....
....

The needs of the customers that will be satisfied are:
....
....

I have chosen this business idea because (advantages and disadvantages):
....
....

What should I learn further to prepare for the business?
....
....

When you have completed the summary of your business idea, you can go on to the next step to start your own business: Prepare a business plan for the proposed business. The Start-Up Mentors training programme can assist you with this. Our programme can help you become more efficient and increase your profit once you have started your business.

If you are still undecided, do not worry!

The purpose of this guidebook is to help you prepare yourself before you start a business. If you do not feel that you are ready at this point to start a business, try to clarify what causes your reticence:

- Are you unsure about your personal capability? Do you think you are not capable of being an entrepreneur?
- Are you unsure about a market with an unmet need that you can fulfill?
- Are you unsure of which idea you want to pursue because you have many ideas that you are considering?
- Are you unsure whether or not you have sufficiently analysed and compared your ideas?

In all cases you now have a better understanding of what it takes to find a good business idea. If you are not ready yet, keep working on it and you will get there! Use the Action Plan form below to list the things that you will do next.

ACTIVITY 14

Action Plan		
Areas that need improvement	What will I do to improve it?	When?

Your next step is to join us for a one-on-one session that you can book on our Facebook page: www.facebook.com/startupmentors

May God bless you and your business.

With love

Xavier K Smith

www.ingramcontent.com/pod-product-compliance
Lightning Source LLC
Chambersburg PA
CBHW081457220526
45466CB00008B/2685